*S*ometimes there is a happening in our lives that changes the way we think about ourselves and sends us along a new path.

These turning points can come when we are young—through a person we meet, an experience we have, a difficulty we overcome.

Since 1789, only forty-two people have been president of the United States. What has made these forty-two people unique? Was there a turning point in their young lives that caused them to change direction and set them on a path that led them to the White House?

—Judith St. George

Note: Forty-two people as president at time of printing.

Posita in hac re veritas est.

Judith St. George

illustrated by

Daniel Powers

Take the Lead, GEORGE WASHINGTON

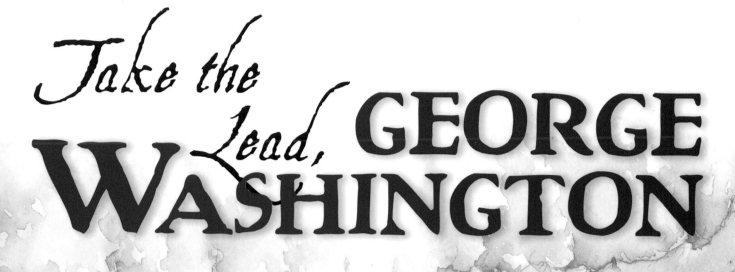

Chapter 1. The Farmer's Son

Right from the start, what George Washington knew best was farms and farming. He was a farmer's son. The Washingtons lived in a small brick farmhouse on Pope's Creek in the British colony of Virginia. And farm life suited George just fine.

George was a busy, curious little boy. His gray-blue eyes took in everything. He watched the family slaves milk the cows (from a safe distance). He chased the chickens, stayed clear of the snippy-snappy geese and played with the kittens in the barn.

What George liked best was to ride horseback around the farm on his father's lap. Augustine Washington—known as Gus—seemed like a giant to George. He was six feet tall and strong. Father and son checked the fields of tobacco. They rode to the family gristmill. Sometimes they visited their neighbors. What a good life!

George was Mary and Gus Washington's first child. He was born on February 22, 1732 (by our calendar). George didn't have his mother and father to himself for long. He had just learned to walk when baby Betty arrived. A year later, baby Samuel was born. Jane, Gus's daughter by his first wife, was part of the family, too. (Gus's first wife had died.) The Washingtons' four-room farmhouse was full of little ones.

Years before, George's father had bought a farm called Epsewasson. It was so big—2,500 acres—that it was called a plantation. When George was three, Gus decided to move his growing family to Epsewasson. George may not have wanted to leave their Pope's Creek farm, but what could he do?

Epsewasson was forty miles north of Pope's Creek. It was a long, bumpy wagon ride. The roads were only rutted trails. Creeks and marshes crisscrossed their route. George held on tight.

The Washingtons' new house was on a bluff overlooking the wide Potomac River. It wasn't much bigger than their Pope's Creek house, but what a handsome spot!

Soon after the family moved, another baby was born—John Augustine. George's sister Jane had died the year before. That made George the oldest of four. No wonder he was happy to escape the full-to-bursting house and play outdoors. Even better was to trail his giant father around the plantation.

Gus Washington hoped to become a wealthy and respected Virginia gentleman. He and the family slaves worked hard growing tobacco. To make money, he became a partner in an iron mine and furnace. That meant more hard work. Gus even did some surveying.

Just before George turned five, his father sailed to England. It was an unhappy day for George. Gus Washington planned to visit Lawrence and Augustine Jr., his two older sons by his first wife. They were in England at Appleby School.

George's father had been born and raised in England. As a boy he had gone to Appleby School, too. Like almost everyone in the American colonies in the 1730s, the Washingtons were British citizens. Gus believed that an English education was important for a gentleman.

Being a gentleman didn't concern George. He was only five. But he knew one day he would go to Appleby School like his brothers.

With his father gone, it was a long winter for George. Mary Washington could hardly read or write, but she had a strong will *and* strong opinions. With her husband away, she was in charge of everything. She gave George lots of orders. Play with the little ones, set an example, stop teasing, don't wake the baby.

Months later, Gus returned. It wasn't soon enough for George. The following year, baby Charles was born. Six-year-old George wasn't surprised. Didn't a new baby arrive every year? But George *was* surprised by another arrival. His twenty-year-old brother, Lawrence Washington, came home from England.

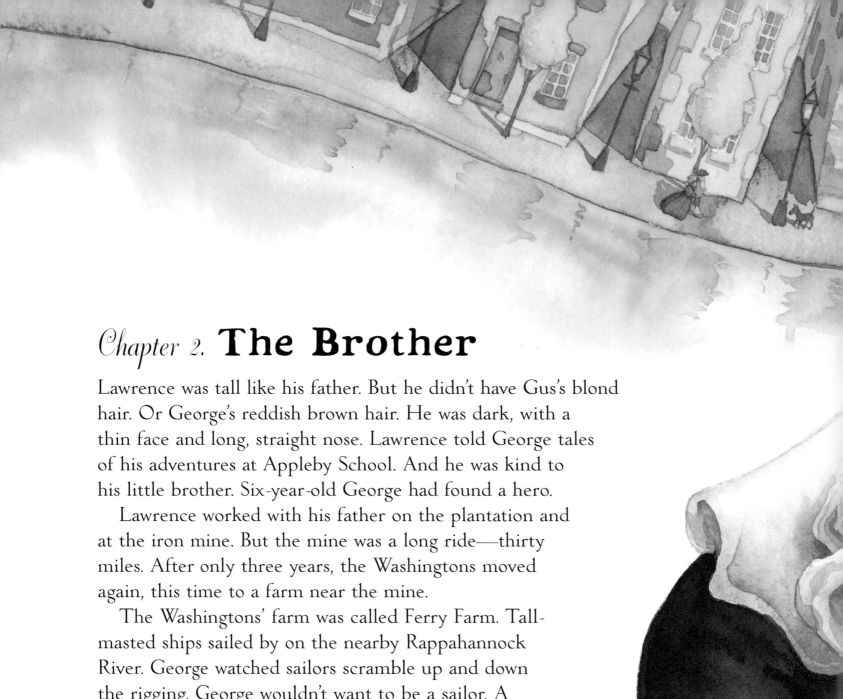

Chapter 2. **The Brother**

Lawrence was tall like his father. But he didn't have Gus's blond hair. Or George's reddish brown hair. He was dark, with a thin face and long, straight nose. Lawrence told George tales of his adventures at Appleby School. And he was kind to his little brother. Six-year-old George had found a hero.

Lawrence worked with his father on the plantation and at the iron mine. But the mine was a long ride—thirty miles. After only three years, the Washingtons moved again, this time to a farm near the mine.

The Washingtons' farm was called Ferry Farm. Tall-masted ships sailed by on the nearby Rappahannock River. George watched sailors scramble up and down the rigging. George wouldn't want to be a sailor. A sailor was at sea for months at a time. Right here on land was good enough for George.

A ferry crossed the river. Sometimes the ferry brought visitors—with playmates for George. Playing Indians and soldiers with wooden tomahawks and swords was the best. But George's mother was strict. "I was ten times more afraid than I ever was of my own parents," a cousin later said of George's mother.

Across the river was Fredericksburg. A town! George had never seen a town before. Buildings were all in a row. People busied themselves up and down the street.

And then George was busy himself. When he turned seven, he started school. An ABC schoolmaster came right to the Washingtons' house. That same year, a baby sister—Mildred—was born. George was more excited about Lawrence joining the army. (It was the British army back then.)

Lawrence was so handsome in his scarlet uniform. Maybe George wouldn't be a gentleman farmer like his father. Maybe he would be a soldier and carry a sword like Lawrence.

Lawrence set sail with the British troops under Admiral Edward Vernon to attack the Spanish in South America. But the British were defeated. And Mildred died. The Washingtons mourned for baby Mildred and worried about Lawrence.

Two years went by. Lawrence wasn't home for George to follow around. He wasn't home to tell George tales of adventure. He wasn't home to help out on the farm. They were hard years. On Christmas Eve, the Ferry Farm house burned down, all but the kitchen. George, his parents, brothers and sister ran out into the night. Flames and sparks shot up into the winter sky. (The house was quickly rebuilt.)

By the time Lawrence returned, George's brother Augustine Jr., known as Austin, had come home. George came to love Austin. But Lawrence was still his hero. Nine Washingtons now filled the house to overflowing. Beds were set up everywhere, even in the parlor. George had almost no space to call his own.

Eleven-year-old George had grown tall and strong. As a farmboy, he had learned to ride early and well. George was like his mother. Mary Washington was plump, but she had always loved to ride.

That spring, George rode some twenty-five miles to visit his cousins. He passed field after field of tobacco that was just greening up. He was on his own. No chores. No nagging. No little ones to pester him.

George had a happy time with his six cousins. They wrestled, raced their horses and held running and leaping contests. George was so big that he easily kept up with his oldest cousins, John and Lawrence. But one afternoon a messenger galloped across the field. George was to return home. Now! His father was dying.

George hurried back to Ferry Farm. He joined his family by his father's bedside in time to hear his father's last words, "I die in peace with all men." George would never forget the date, April 12, 1743. At least George still had Lawrence. He could always count on Lawrence.

Chapter 3. A Proper Virginia Gentleman

George missed his gentle father. His mother had a pleasant voice, but she didn't always speak to George in a pleasant way. And one day she told him that there wasn't enough money to send him to Appleby School. George was crushed.

Instead, George went to a little nearby school run by a neighbor, Mr. Hobby. He studied arithmetic, geography, literature and Latin. He never cared much for books or reading. His favorite subject? Arithmetic, by far.

George began to keep copybooks. He decorated the pages with fancy letters and drawings of maps and trees. But George was practical. He didn't write down his thoughts or hopes or even what he did that day. He filled his books with arithmetic problems. He also copied deeds and wills and other legal papers.

George's father had always wanted to be a Virginia gentleman. George wanted to be a gentleman, too. And if he couldn't learn to be a gentleman at Appleby School, then he would teach himself. George copied a whole book on good manners.

Some made sense: "In visiting the Sick, do not play the Physician." Some were silly: "Cleanse not your teeth with the Table Cloth, Napkin, Fork or Knife." One hundred and ten rules in all. He copied every one.

Lawrence took over as George's substitute father. Lawrence thought that the British navy would make a fine career for fourteen-year-old George. George didn't like the sea. Or want to be a sailor. But Lawrence knew best. This time George's mother saved the day. She wouldn't hear of it.

George was the third-oldest son. His father's will didn't leave him much, just Ferry Farm, some Fredericksburg property and ten slaves, with his mother controlling all of it until he was twenty-one. Second son Austin was given George's birthplace, the Pope's Creek farm. Oldest son Lawrence got the prize—Epsewasson. Right away he changed the name to Mount Vernon after his old commander, Admiral Edward Vernon.

Years before, George had liked living at Epsewasson with his family.
Now he liked it even better as Mount Vernon. Lawrence was there.
And Lawrence had built a new nine-room house. To escape his mother's
constant do-this, do-that, George visited Lawrence whenever he could.

Lawrence was becoming a proper Virginia gentleman. He was a
skilled horseman, a careful businessman and a loyal friend. People liked
Lawrence, and Lawrence liked people. And he always knew what to say
to young women. George *never* knew what to say to young women.
George wanted to be just like Lawrence someday.

By the time he was fifteen, George's school days were over. But
he found his father's old surveying tools for measuring land—a
sixty-six-foot-long iron chain and a transit with a telescope
and compass. Surveying was mostly mathematics, and
mathematics was what George did best.

George and surveying were a perfect match. He liked working in the hot Virginia sun. He liked taking exact measurements and running straight lines. How many acres was Ferry Farm? How wide was the Rappahannock River? George even measured Lawrence's turnip field. And he earned money as a surveyor's assistant. Coins jingling in his pocket made a pleasant sound.

At fifteen George was broad-shouldered, straight-backed, taller than most men, and a fine rider. Fox hunting was his specialty. Lawrence made sure that George took dancing lessons. George's feet were extra-large, but he was a good dancer.

George had all the makings of a Virginia gentleman like Lawrence. But Ferry Farm, ten slaves and some Fredericksburg property wouldn't ever bring him wealth. He would have to make his own way in the world.

Chapter 4. **The Fairfax Connection**

Lawrence found himself a wife. He married Anne Fairfax, the daughter of Lawrence's wealthy neighbor, Colonel William Fairfax. George was lucky. He often visited Colonel Fairfax's "great house," Belvoir, with Lawrence and Anne. It was a handsome brick house surrounded by outbuildings.

And George made a new friend—Anne's brother, George William, whom he called Mr. Fairfax. George William was seven years older than George, but that didn't seem to matter.

George admired Anne's father. Colonel Fairfax was an outdoorsman, like George. He rode for miles every day, overseeing his estate. He led fox hunts and raced his horses. At night he played cards and billiards . . . and often won. George was good at cards and billiards, too.

George wasn't much of a talker, but he was a good listener. He was charmed by the talk at Belvoir. Talk was about tobacco, horses, gambling, fox hunting, food, wine and military service. Most of all, talk was about land, especially western wilderness frontier land.

The more George heard, the more he liked the idea of buying land someday. Then he could have his own plantation and "great house." He would fox hunt and travel to Williamsburg for the theater, balls and gambling. Maybe he'd even join the military like Lawrence and Colonel Fairfax.

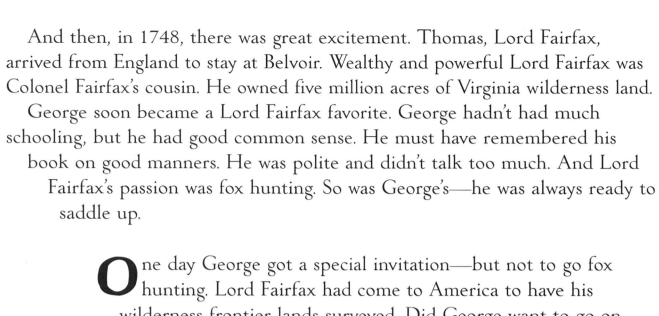

And then, in 1748, there was great excitement. Thomas, Lord Fairfax, arrived from England to stay at Belvoir. Wealthy and powerful Lord Fairfax was Colonel Fairfax's cousin. He owned five million acres of Virginia wilderness land. George soon became a Lord Fairfax favorite. George hadn't had much schooling, but he had good common sense. He must have remembered his book on good manners. He was polite and didn't talk too much. And Lord Fairfax's passion was fox hunting. So was George's—he was always ready to saddle up.

One day George got a special invitation—but not to go fox hunting. Lord Fairfax had come to America to have his wilderness frontier lands surveyed. Did George want to go on the survey trip? Colonel Fairfax's son, George William, was going. If George decided to go, his pay would be $7.20 a day. $7.20 a day! George could already hear coins jingling in his pockets. What was there to decide? He could do simple surveys. He was good at mathematics. His handwriting was neat and clear for keeping survey notes. Plus, it was the perfect chance to learn more about surveying. Best of all, he would be on his own for a month. His answer? YES.

As a young Virginia gentleman, George wore stylish clothes. (But they weren't very sturdy.) He could ride for hours without getting tired. (But he always came home to a hot meal and a soft bed.) He told time by a pocket watch. (Not by the sun like a woodsman.) He thought of himself as an outdoorsman. (But he had never taken on the wilderness.)

At sixteen, George was more than six feet tall, as strong as a man and already shaving. It didn't concern him one bit that the survey party would ride hundreds of miles and live in the wilderness. The trip couldn't start soon enough.

Chapter 5. The Greatest Adventure

George bought a notebook for his trip. He titled it *Journey over the Mountains.*
This was going to be the greatest adventure of his life.

George and his friend George William Fairfax rode out on March 11, 1748.
The next day they met up with the head surveyor, James Genn.

The three of them made their way over the rolling Blue Ridge Mountains
by way of Ashby Gap. Below stretched miles and miles of fertile countryside—
the Shenandoah Valley. What a beautiful sight!

James Genn picked up his four helpers. They made their first survey. In a
marsh. In the rain. George was soaked and covered with mud. That was all
right. He'd wash up later.

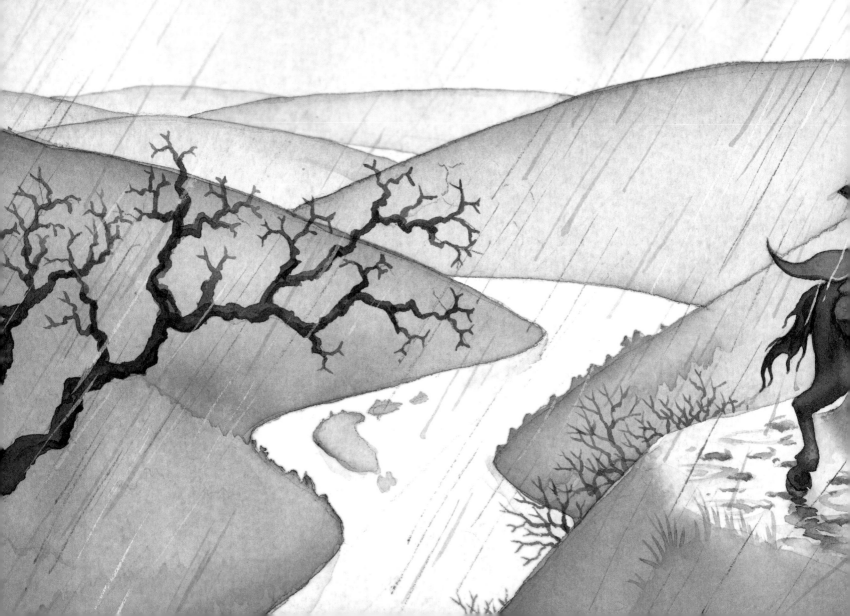

That night they roomed at Isaac Pennington's . . . with no place to wash up.
George took off his clothes and climbed into bed. The mattress was dirty straw.
The blanket was crawling with fleas and lice. Polite as always, he waited until
Isaac Pennington left the room. Then he jumped out of bed and lay on the
floor for the night. At least George didn't lose his temper. (He sometimes did.)

The rain never let up. If their party couldn't find shelter, they slept in a tent.
It leaked. They cooked over a sputtering fire. They surveyed between down-
pours. It was hard to keep the survey notes dry.

When they came to the South Branch of the Potomac River, it was flooded. They would camp out until the water fell. George was wet and miserable for two days. At last, James Genn gave the order: Everyone ride across the river.

Ride across? But that was dangerous. The water was swift and icy cold. Branches and logs tumbled by. Dangerous or not, George had no choice.

George spurred his horse into the rushing river. Right away, the current swept the frightened animal downstream. He was frantic. He heaved and rocked to keep his head above water. Both George and his horse could drown. They needed help. But everyone else was struggling to cross the river, too.

Mathematics. Geometry. Angles. *Cross the river at an angle*. George pressed his knees into his horse's flanks. He pulled hard on the reins to turn him upstream. The horse balked. Then he began to swim for the opposite shore. Slowly, he made headway. Then his hooves touched bottom. He scrambled up the slippery bank. They'd made it—but barely.

Surely the others would stop to catch their breath and dry off. No, they wanted to reach Thomas Cresap's trading post before dark. It was a forty-mile ride. The trail was blocked by fallen trees. The rain came down in torrents.

"The Worst Road that was ever trod by Man or Beast," George complained in his journal.

For the next four days, they were trapped by the rain at Cresap's trading post. And then a war party of thirty Indian braves showed up—with a scalp. The Indians built a fire, played their drums and rattles and danced a wild war dance.

That night George wrote everything down in his journal by the light of the trading-post fire. He was so fascinated that he spent the next day with the Indians, too.

The survey party pushed on to Patterson's Creek. James Genn told the men to swim their horses across. Patterson's Creek wasn't as wide or as swollen as the South Branch had been. But it was fast-moving and filled with broken branches.

George fought down panic. How had he done it the last time? At an angle. George gripped the reins tight to show that he was in charge. His horse responded. It was as if he trusted George to get them across safely. And he did.

George was wet and cold. He'd been wet and cold for days. He would soon be returning to Ferry Farm. Maybe he should return now. Who could fault him if he did? George didn't hesitate long. He had agreed to come . . . and was being paid. That was that. Wet and cold or not, he would stick it out.

Chapter 6. The Woodsman

The surveying began in earnest. Open meadows were the easiest. Trees got in the way of measuring distances. Slogging through marshes wasn't much better. The mud almost sucked George's boots off. What luck he'd packed two pairs!

George became the company's tree expert. Trees marked boundary lines. And were markers for measuring. A large chestnut . . . two sugar maples . . . a black walnut. George knew them all. The survey crew counted on him.

James Genn counted on George, too. Fetch my camp chest. Set up the transit. Write down these figures. George even ran out the sixty-six-foot-long chain and took measurements.

George's spirits picked up. He was doing all right. Better than all right. He was gaining respect for himself. He could have turned back and gone home. But he hadn't. The rain hadn't stopped him, either. He'd become a working member of the crew.

Mucking through marshes, sleeping in a leaky tent and eating half-cooked meals didn't get any easier. Nevertheless, George tried to make them *seem* easier, at least to himself. He'd take on the wilderness and weather at an angle like those two rivers he'd forded. No more complaints, not even in his journal. And he'd do his best to ignore the rain.

Actually, the rain had done him a favor. If their party hadn't been trapped by the rain at Cresap's trading post, he wouldn't have met up with those Indians. He would never forget them.

George was soon tested. Twice the tent blew down while they were sleeping. One night it filled with campfire smoke. Another night the straw they slept on caught fire. Each time George and the others had to bed down outdoors.

George made the best of it. And the best of it was that outdoor sleeping was a pleasant surprise. When it didn't rain, thousands of stars studded the night sky. A shooting star flashed overhead. But George made sure to keep the camp-fire going. Roaming packs of wolves were too close for comfort. George never had much luck with his rifle. What if he shot at a wolf and missed?

Though the rains came down day after
day, the crew continued to go from survey to survey.
They urged their horses up steep and slippery mountain
trails. They traveled single file along rock ledges. They crossed
narrow creeks and streams. George often brought up the rear.
But he never dropped behind. And wonder of all wonders, the
sun came out from time to time.

George looked around . . . when he could. The country was all misty
meadows, rich, fertile soil, giant stands of balsam and spruce trees, water-
falls, hidden coves and hollows. *This* was where he'd buy land someday.

Then it was back home for George and George William. They took a
wrong turn and rode an extra twenty miles. "We had lost ourselves," George
confessed. They also saw a rattlesnake. In his journal, George wrote,
"Rattled Snake."

George's thirty-three days in the wilderness were over. He was happy to eat a hot meal and sleep in a soft bed, *but* he now knew he could do without them.

He still carried a watch, but he'd learned to tell time like a woodsman by the sun . . . when it came out. He'd ridden endless hours in the rain, slept in wet clothes and cooked over open fires. He'd worked as part of a crew, followed orders, tested his strength and kept his head in times of danger.

George was on his way to being a proper Virginia gentleman like Lawrence. Once that had been enough. But why not try for something more? After all, he'd gone beyond Lawrence *and* his father. On his own, he'd broken into the western frontier and proved himself. And liked it. The open, land-rich American frontier was in his blood forever.

Sixteen-year-old George didn't know what lay ahead. Maybe it would catch him by surprise the way the wilderness had caught him by surprise. Well, he had met the challenge of the wilderness. He would do his best to meet the next challenge, too, whatever it might be.

And that was a promise.

GEORGE WASHINGTON BIOGRAPHY

Born in a Westmoreland County farmhouse on February 22, 1732 (by our calendar), in the British colony of Virginia, George Washington had little formal education. His father died when he was eleven. By the time Washington was fifteen, he had finished his schooling and begun working as a surveyor's assistant.

Washington joined the British militia in 1753, defending Virginia's borders and serving on the western frontier during the French and Indian War. A year after resigning from the militia in 1758, he married Martha Custis, a wealthy widow. They soon made their home at Mount Vernon, the plantation which Washington's brother Lawrence had left him in his will.

As a member of the Virginia House of Burgesses, Washington served as a delegate to the First and Second Continental Congresses. In 1775 he was elected commander-in-chief of the Continental army.

With untrained troops and little financial support, for the next six years Washington fought the British to secure American independence. He won daring victories, as well as suffering devastating defeats. In 1778, the French joined the American cause, the combined forces finally defeating the British in 1781.

But Washington was not to enjoy retirement. As delegate, and then as president of the Constitutional Convention, which convened to write a new constitution, Washington was unanimously elected president of the United States in 1789.

President Washington faced and resolved numerous challenges: to organize a government and establish a cabinet, tackle severe financial problems, develop better

relations with Great Britain and negotiate treaties with Indian tribes. In 1792, he was elected to a second term, once again unanimously.

In 1797, Washington retired to his beloved Mount Vernon. He died there on December 14, 1799. Known as the Father of His Country, George Washington became a legend in his own time, guiding the nation through its first difficult years with a deft and steady hand and putting his permanent stamp on the presidency.

BIBLIOGRAPHY

Andrist, Ralph K., ed. *George Washington: A Biography in His Own Words*. Vol. 1. New York: Newsweek, Inc., 1972.

Cunliffe, Marcus. *George Washington: Man and Monument*. Boston: Little, Brown and Company, 1958.

Fisher, Ron. *Blue Ridge Range: The Gentle Mountains*. Washington, D.C.: National Geographic Society, 1992.

Fitzpatrick, John C., ed. *The Writings of George Washington from the Original Manuscript Sources*. Vol. 1. Washington, D.C.: United States Printing Office, 1931.

Flexner, James Thomas. *George Washington: The Forge of Experience (1732–1775)*. Boston: Little, Brown and Company, 1965.

Flexner, James Thomas. *Washington: The Indispensable Man*. Boston: Little, Brown and Company, 1974.

Freeman, Douglas Southall. *George Washington: A Biography*. Vol. 1. New York: Charles Scribner's Sons, 1948.

Jackson, Donald, ed. *The Diaries of George Washington*. Vol. 1, 1748–1765. Charlottesville: University Press of Virginia, 1976.

Morison, Samuel Eliot. *The Young Man Washington*. Cambridge, Massachusetts: Harvard University Press, 1932.

Warren, Jack. "The Childhood of George Washington." *Northern Neck of Virginia Historical Magazine* (December 1999): 5785–5809.

Wilson, Woodrow. *George Washington*. New York: Harper & Brothers Publishers, 1903.

For my friend and editor, Patti Gauch.   —J.St.G.

To Josie, for instilling in me an acute curiosity about history. And to Silke.   —D.P.

PRÆFECTUS POSTERUS

Patricia Lee Gauch, editor

PHILOMEL BOOKS,
a division of Penguin Young Readers Group, 345 Hudson Street, New York, NY 10014.
Philomel Books, Reg. U.S. Pat. & Tm. Off. The scanning, uploading and distribution of this book via the Internet
or via any other means without the permission of the publisher is illegal and punishable by law.
Please purchase only authorized electronic editions, and do not participate in or encourage electronic
piracy of copyrighted materials. Your support of the author's rights is appreciated.
Published simultaneously in Canada.
Manufactured in China by South China Printing Co. Ltd.
Designed by Semadar Megged.   Text set in 16.5-point Pastonchi.
The illustrations are rendered in watercolor on Arches paper.
Library of Congress Cataloging-in-Publication Data
St. George, Judith, date.
Take the lead, George Washington / by Judith St. George ; illustrated by Daniel Powers.
p. cm.   Includes bibliographical references. 1. Washington, George, 1732–1799—Childhood and
youth—Juvenile literature. 2. Presidents—United States—Biography—Juvenile literature.
I. Powers, Daniel, ill. II. Title.   E312.66.S75 2005   973.4'1'092—dc22   2004006734
ISBN 0-399-23887-5
1 3 5 7 9 10 8 6 4 2
First Impression